POEMS AND PRAYERS -THE HIP-HOP WAY!

Written by
Trancy Custis AKA TBone Snackz

Foreword by Arnita Custis

Poems and Prayers – The Hip Hop Way!
Copyright © 2010 by Trancy Custis AKA Tbone Snackz, Arnita Custis, Sheila Hayford, What A Word Publishing and Media Group

Published by: Sheila Hayford, What A Word Publishing and Media Group
P. O. Box 371
Camden, DE 19934
U.S.A.
www.whatawordpublishing.com

All rights reserved. No part of this book may be reproduced or transmitted in any form or by any means without written permission from the Publisher. Permission requests should be sent to What A Word Publishing and Media Group
Attn: Sheila Hayford
P. O. Box 371
Camden, DE 19934
U.S.A.
Permission requests may also be sent via email to info@whatawordpublishing.com

ISBN 978-0-692-01401-1

Printed in the United States of America

DEDICATIONS

This book is dedicated to:

Adrian, Trancy's mother: Without you none of this would have been possible. I thank God for giving me life through my mother and the chance for me to express these poems to my readers and listeners. Thank you

Mildred Spence, Arnita's grandmother: You're a wonderful grandmother. Thanks for encouraging Trancy with his poems

And to Kema, Chaiyonna, Tommy, Amaya and De`asia: You make us feel we are the most fortunate parents in the world!

Trancy and Arnita Custis

ACKNOWLEDGEMENTS

We would first like to acknowledge our Lord and our God, Jesus Christ, who has saved us and given meaning to our lives. We thank God Almighty for giving us the grace and the talents to write this book. And we thank you, our readers, for taking the time to buy and read this book. We hope you enjoy our unique style of poems. May your life be blessed.

Tracy Custis AKA Tbone Snackz
Arnita Custis

FOREWORD

I am pleased to introduce you to Trancy's poems. Trancy is a wonderful husband and father, and as you can see, he likes to write. In the first section, Trancy writes about the difficult tests and challenges he endured. In the next section he writes about his family and has shared some of the poems he wrote about his loving wife. And in the last section he shares his prayers to God. Below is my poem to Trancy. May you be blessed and find fulfillment in sharing the talents God has given you with others.

Husband: You're So Special!

Before you came in my life
I prayed God would send me a good man
And when He did, there came you!
I knew you were the one
That was part of His plan
I had to have you
And when I met you
It took all of my hurt and pain away
You made me feel like a lady again
That's why you're so special to me
You gave me a smile again
Every night you would hold me in your arms
I felt safe; didn't have to worry about no harm
You made me a happy woman
When you gave me a beautiful daughter
You're not just my husband; you're my best friend
I love the way you put a smile on my face each day

By Arnita Custis

LIFE WAS FULL OF TESTS AND TRIALS

Walk With Me

Take a walk with me
Sit down and talk with me
No lights on
Sit in the dark with me
Got a lot on my mind
Pain all in my heart
I feel like crying
A lot of bad things done happened to me
I ain't lying
Been struggling all my life
Still having bad dreams
I've been through it all
But it seems like I'm still paying the price
Trying to figure out what's wrong and what's right
Twenty-seven years I've been staying strong
If God didn't want me here I wouldn't belong
So why was everybody treating me wrong
I still play it in my head
That same song
Still struggling out here on my own
Going through life I got treated bad
I'm supposed to be happy so why am I sad
I'm scared from the pain
I'm going insane
It was so bad couldn't remember my own name
Just sitting here having a conversation with God
Getting all emotional, tears rolling from my eyes
Dropped to my knees praying for a better life
I know I'm not perfect, I ain't even living right
You answered my prayers when you sent me a wife
Now I can rest peacefully and call it a night

By Trancy Custis AKA Tbone Snackz

They Said I wouldn't make it in Life

When I was growing up people told me I was going to be nothing
Twenty-eight years later I am bumping bass and all that
Can't take my style from me
No fitted hats: - only black doo rags
Always talking about they got more than me
He didn't know I had the same stuff he did
You can tell by his face; look at him-he's mad
Don't point fingers at me 'cos your mom separated from your dad
I ain't to blame if he wasn't treating her right
Some things don't stay the same
He thought she would come back so he bought her a ring
She said she couldn't go through no more of that pain
Couldn't take it no more
Everything's changed; I know I ain't that great
Feels like I was trapped and someone was locking the gate
Ain't playing no more, you can tell by the look on my face
I did a lot of things in my days and still remember the place
I didn't think I belong here
Tell me what am I doing wrong?
Going crazy like I was losing my mind
Trying to take my own life but it wasn't my time
Tbone Snackz is my name
That's what you're going to hear all the time
They told me I wasn't going to survive
Got to be 'cos of my two little girls
So I stand here, spit in the face of you haters
Can't keep me down
Catch you later

By Trancy Custis AKA Tbone Snackz

Letter to God

Why do I go through so much pain?
And everything around me still feels the same?
Fingers pointing at me as if I'm the blame
Why do I still feel sad when I'm supposed to grin?
Why do I still hold all my pain?
I just want to know why I am emotional like I want to cry
Just don't feel good on the inside
Asking all these questions: God why?
Got a sickness that's messing with my eyes
It just makes me sick that I am going through all this pain
Just need a healing prayer for a change
Don't want my situation to be the same
Going crazy like I was going insane
Seems like time after time I want to flip
Grab the Xbox controller
Play the game and don't even trip
I'm on both of my knees God, praying for a fix
Need a different life; tired of going through all this

By Trancy Custis AKA Tbone Snackz

Separated from my Mother

You weren't there when I was taken into foster care
I cried every night telling myself this situation wasn't right
Tears rolling down my eyes as they put me in a place
Didn't have a chance to say goodbye; I wish I could
Where I'm at now, life's not good
Without you I can't move on
I tried to keep my head up and be strong
Seems like the days kept getting long
I got mistreated, It was so wrong

Praying to God to put me where I belong
A lot of things changed; I am different now
It's not the same 'cos of all the pain
I felt so alone
I couldn't even talk to my mom on the phone
Three years came to past; I'm finally home at last
Got my problems behind me
I was heart broken that my family couldn't find me
I'm smiling 'cos things are looking up
That part of my life was rough

By Trancy Custis AKA Tbone Snackz

I just wanna say "Thank You"

Lord, I just wanna thank you for giving me life
Even though my situations weren't even right
I never gave up
Every day I had to put up, Ah! Fight
The devil had me under his wings
Whispering in my ear all the bad things
I thought my world was coming to an end
From all the pain
I dropped to my knees
I called out one name –"God"
I know you hear me 'cos You heard my cries
I want to change
Don't want to be known as "that" guy
Couldn't talk to nobody
No one understood my life
Just talking to You, God, made everything alright
You even told me You would forgive me of my sins
I used to smile but they took away my grin
I felt lost but with God I know I am going to win

Seemed like no one cared, I was all lonely
That's what I used to feel
But since I found God I know everything in God is real

By Trancy Custis AKA Tbone Snackz

I'm looking for God and you can't stop me

My life's about to change
I'm tired of doing the same ol' thing
I've been hearing You, God
You keep calling my name
Since I found You I don't' have no more pain
You taught me how to forgive and forget
There's still stuff in my life I haven't done yet
You said patience is the key
That what most people lack, not me
I stay in chill mode
That's why I stay relaxed
With my feet up rocking in a black wave cap
When I was young I was never taught how to love
But God showed me the way, watching me from above
As long as I stay committed nothing can go wrong
Just got to keep my head up and stay strong
I was down before
Now I'm where I belong
A lot of years
I've been shedding tears
A lot of pain in my heart I kept right there
Through it all I'm still here
In the beginning I was confused
I know what I know now, I know what to do
People kept testing me wanting me to blow fuse
I decide my life; they can't tell me what to do
Still wondering why some want my downfall

They want me in a corner with my back against the wall
One thing about it: they can never stop my shine
As long as God's got my back, I'll cross that finish line

By Trancy Custis AKA TBone Snackz

I'm just trying to find myself

I'm lost right now trying to find myself
All confused still lying to myself
Still putting myself in certain situations
A lot of things done happened to me that I never mentioned
Think about all the stuff I done wrong
I pretty much hate myself
Got a lot of stuff on my chest
That I just can't shake myself
Always kept my head up so I'm swallowing my pride
All messed up in my head
I'm still a cool guy
I always stood my own ground
So you've got to believe me
Don't care what you think about me
Take it or leave it
I know when I was young
All I did was get mistreated
My attitude now just gets the best of me
Smoking and drinking put a lot of stress on me
I couldn't understand why I couldn't get love at home
The way I was treated growing up was just so wrong
I didn't talk about it
Nowadays just express it in my poems
I smile a lot, who am I kidding?
Just an emotional guy who seems to hide feelings
I'm a grown man now
Still feels like I don't feel no love

I'm in the struggle by myself
So I'm continuing to fight the good fight
Trying to fix my situation so I can experience the good life
It feels like I am getting back my senses
Like I've been trapped for years hiding behind fences
I still got a lot of stuff to improve
I'm starting to feel good about myself
I'm going out of this world as that cool dude
That's why I'm happy about my life now
Ain't worrying about stressing
As long as the Lord's in my heart
I'm just waiting on my blessing

By Trancy Custis AKA Tbone Snackz

Gotta Learn to Love Myself

I'm twenty-eight years now
Gotta learn to love myself
Nobody's going to do that for me
So I gotta protect my health
When I was an infant I had to learn how to crawl and walk
Got a lot to say that's why I'm a talking
 I'm loved by many but hated by most of y'all
Only time I'll trip is if my shoes are untied
But I'll never fall in the truth
Everything I speak is real
Blind people can't see me but they know I'm here
Ever since I was young I've seen a lot of things
Kept a lot of stuff in that's causing me a lot of pain
Seen a lot of crazy stuff in my time
Like some of the stories you've been watching on "Lifetime"
Got a lot of sunny days ahead and my future is so bright
Why is my situation so tight?
And everything around me just don't seem right
Just believe in yourself 'cos nobody else will

Thought about death
Popping sixty pills took the thought outta my head and my mouth
It was making me ill
You're always going to see me on the move 'cos I can't sit still
It's only a matter of time before my name becomes a franchise
It wasn't when I was young
But I'm about to come up as the sunrise

By Trancy Custis AKA Tbone Snackz

A Birthday Wish

On my birthday thinking what I wanted to wish for
Every year done past me by
I want more
Just want something I can be thankful for
Wish I had a different life
Take me back in time and make everything right
Wish you would change some of my ways
So I wouldn't have to go through none of them bad days
Wish I never lost my grandmother
Wanted her to still be here
Through this day and time
Wish I never went through that pain
So I wouldn't have to walk through the storm and the rain
Wish I never got abused
Looking at my body and seeing the bruise
The things done happen now, what am I supposed to do?
Wish none of them ever came true
Wish it could have been brighter
The only thing I wish for now is
Never again to go through that pain

By Trancy Custis AKA Tbone Snackz

A Different Life Ahead Of Me

I'm on the road cruising; that means I stay on the go
I'm not bowling when I say I'm in the lanes, I know
I 'm not perfect, got responsibilities
So I can take some of the blame
Had some people who tried to control my life
It's up to me to make everything right
People used to treat me wrong, ain't even right
I ain't in this world to do no Impressing
Y'all still guessing but I'm the one that's still stressing
Twenty-eight years of my life I sat back and got taught a lesson
God was on my side
The whole time He threw me some blessings
Change is coming
That's what I'm about
Just got to live it out
Struggled my whole life
Know what tough times are all about
Grandparents taught me all about respect
You can't tell me I ain't got one
You ain't heard a disrespectful thing come out my mouth
Jack, don't let nobody control you
My grandma taught me that
Seems like my life is still in park
No lights on, I'm still sitting in the dark
Just sitting here looking for the switch
With both my hands together praying for a fix

By Trancy Custis AKA Tbone Snackz

A Lot Of Things On My Mind

What should I do? Time is running out
My life choices got to be made
Rubber on the tires are burning out trying to travel
Don't care who don't like me
All they're going to do is hate
But you know I can relate
Got to get going; ain't trying to be late
Highways are always full
Need to slow down ain't trying to get pulled
Ran into a lot of like problems filled with bull
Had to change a lot of my ways
That's why I took a detour
A lot of things I did were my fault
Say what you want, I call them your thoughts
Don't try to judge me, you don't know what I been
Though sitting here trying to figure out my next move
You better trust and believe
I never gave up; I always believed in me
Like I was short of feelings
Like I couldn't breathe
Struggling to figure a lot of stuff out
If you were never in that position then you don't know what I'm talking about

By Trancy Custis AKA Tbone Snackz

All I'm Trying To Do Is Survive

Trying to survive in this world
So what if I struggle into the end
I'll always be me
So forget friends
I was born by myself

I don't need none of them
They only come around you when you got cash to spend
I don't need those no good friends
Most females trip me out saying they want a good man
Soon as they get one they treat him wrong
Listening to their no good girlfriends
When you do it to them
Dey don't like it
That's when stuff hit the fan
They trip me out praying for a good man
Let me tell you something –
I'm all about mine
If a girl is on that ball, save it
I ain't got the time
They say love is blind
Need a girl that's gonna be real
Not the one that always be lying
God told me everything gonna be alright
He even threw me signs
He told me to take it one day at a time
I'm just waiting patiently on my day to shine
How can I find myself in situations where I have to
Put up a fight
I know every relationship got problems
Tell me what I'm not doing right
Maybe I need to step away from the devil and
Stand in God's light
I don't like the way I'm living
Just need a different life
Tired of the pain and tears and the bad things I'd done for years
I just need to change
God I need your help
That's why I been calling
On Your name

By Trancy Custis AKA Tbone Snackz

Can't Understand If You Ain't Never Been There

You would think I'm a wrestler
The way I've been going through the ropes
You would think I'm a fein the way people said
I was strung out on dope
There's some stuff about me that they still don't know
Since a youngin' I done sat back
Watched a lot of stuff
I don't trust nobody, my life was rough
Don't have friends either; life was tough
I'd rather ride alone 'cos going through a lot of stuff
Don't need nobody
Stayed to myself
That's the way I feel
Tear the roads up, shifting the gears
Look into my eyes, you don't see any fear
This is my life
You ain't been through the pain
People can't understand my life
Feel my pain, put your feet in my shoes
Then you'll understand what I mean
Got put into a situation where there was no love
My life was just rough
Being the black sheep was so messed up
Tried to change it wasn't no luck
All I'm trying to do is chill
Letting you know what it is real ...

By Trancy Custis AKA Tbone Snackz

Change Is coming; Follow Me

Yo! The name is Trancy Custis
Everything's about to change
I'm still the same person, nothing seemed to have changed
I'm always doing my own thing trying to live life
Better now without the headaches and pains
Ain't got nothing to lose no more
Just everything to gain
When it rains it pours; see myself doing good
Enjoying life even more
I'm leaving everything in the Lord God's hand
He's bigger than me; just got to ignore man
How do you tell me I don't have respect?
Trancy's the coolest around you ever met
Trying to focus on myself, to get my life back on track
Used to be on top, fell a couple steps back
Learned from my mistakes
Just gotta bounce back
I'm in this world trying to make moves
Doing different things; my life's got to improve
I'm weighing out all my options
Trying to better myself
It feels like I'm lost when there's nothing left
Yeah, I took a lot of heat in my life
Have God on my side now so I know everything is right
Remember when I said: tired of living life
Just couldn't take it
Done being through it all
But in the end I still made it
When I'm going through my problems
I just look up in the sky
I know where to find all my answers
That's why I'm having a conversation with God who knows all my pain
That's why I'm not scared to cry

If people only knew what I hold on the inside
Nobody understands me but God…..

By Trancy Custis AKA Tbone Snackz

Continue To Hold On

I got a funny feeling it's so deep inside
I get angry at myself some things I can't hide
The pains beating me up on the inside
Holding my tears back so I won't cry
Used to tell people about all the stuff I see
My mom said don't worry about it
But why is this happening to me
I just wanted this to be over
Even thought about suicide
I can't go that way
Got too much pride
Just want to go away
Talking to God
Hoping will make it one day
As I'm sitting here on the floor
I'm down like I can't get up anymore
Like my strength is gone
Feels like I'm weak
But I'm going to continue to stay strong

By: Trancy Custis AKA Tbone Snackz

Don't Care What You say About Me

I'm a different dude, some things changed
Still got the same attitude; don't play me for a fool
All I'm trying to do is remain cool
People trippin' me out
Stay in your own lane
A six letter word and it is called change
Don't need turn signals for me to cross over into your lane
There were times in my life when stuff didn't matter
Not now
I'm grown, got goals
So I got to climb the ladder
Experienced a lot of good things and some bad things
I done went through everything
Just trying to forget my pains
I liked my life just the way it was
Couple years ago I could have been gone
Didn't do nothing wrong
Just was in a situation where I didn't belong
Thanks to God I can continue my life on
Throw the head phones on
Listen to that same song
God still wanted me here
If he didn't I would have been through
I've seen a lot of stuff through the years
Though I been through it all I'm still here
Look in my eyes you don't see no fear
I feel so great
Got a lot on my mind
Like I've been trapped for years trying to find an escape
Now in my life I can say I'm free
Lifting both of my hands up
Telling God: Come take me

By: Trancy Custis AKA Tbone Snackz

Feels Like I Done Lost Myself

Just a fresh young man; a lot of haters around me
I'll be a fool if they take my last breath
Don't blame me 'cos your life's a mess
I'm on top of my game
Continue with my steps
I'm a child of God so you know that I'm blessed
Didn't need any help
If I got into trouble, that was on myself
Remember going outside walking up and down the streets
No fear in me; my heart never skipped a beat
If you've seen what I seen
Bodies fallen at your feet
Some people didn't like me 'cos I spoke my mind
Candy man right in the hood hustling; had my own grind
People would say this about me and that
Telling nothing but lies
I haven't been the same since grandpa and grandma died
People want to know why I feel I like I'm in control
My Grandma told me to take charge: I'm doing as I was told
I ain't trying to put too much on my chest
A lot of things that went on in my life took me through a lot of stress
I'm strong now, it's me at my best
All my life I done paid the cast
I didn't know who I was anymore, I felt lost
Didn't listen to anybody growing up; felt like I was my own boss
Didn't make good decisions that was my fault
You gotta learn from your mistakes and find a way out
I tried to escape, guess it was because I didn't find no love
Feels like I done lost myself
Just because I know God's angels were watching
I'm the man in my life
I stand my ground again

By Trancy Custis AKA Tbone Snackz

Getting Through My Pain

Let's get through all of my tough times
You were there through all of my hard times
Not once did you ever leave me stuck
You stood by my side that's what you call love
Even when I was facing a lot of depression
You told me don't worry about nothing but I kept on stressing
I couldn't figure out what was going on
I know what I had to do to stay strong
Even in my darkest fears it was faith that kept me here
I kept my head down when something went wrong
I'm better than that
I got to keep holding on
You were there to even hold my hand
Told me it would get better; just keep on praying
I never gave up hope
Life teaches you different things
If you keep holding on you'll never change
You were there with me to experience everything
Now I've got a different outlook on life
I want to thank you for the advice

By Trancy Custis AKA Tbone Snackz

Overcoming My Pain

Growing up I was a troubled kid
Trying to live life the way it Is
Went through a lot of ups and downs
Waiting on my life to turn around
Like I was lost, just waiting to be found
Chose my own path, stood my own ground
Trying to figure out why my life was bad

No smiles, I was feeling all sad
Just sitting here thinking to myself
The problems I'm going through, nobody to blame but myself
I'm trapped like I can't get out
Life all messed up, I can't figure it out
Telling myself: why does this hurt?
So much talking to God
Telling Him I've already been through enough
He told me everything will work out for the good
I'm still praying about it
Wish I would change it if I could
My situation seem like it was no good
Went through it all my life like there's no change
I'm tired of hurting, take away some of my pain
Just want to get a lot of pain off my chest
The more I get it off, the better I can rest

By: Trancy Custis AKA Tbone Snackz

There's Something Still Missing

I just don't feel right; head still banging
Done said everything I could out of my mouth
People still don't understand what I'm saying
It must be a game to y'all I
Look at my face, can't you tell that I ain't playing?
I'm still in the game
Got love for everybody, respect still the same
Trying to be a nice guy but what do you get out of life?
Did what I was supposed to, it almost cost me my life
Took a lot to change, the only thing I switched up was my nickname
It don't matter if I was doing good or bad, my pain is still the same
Don't come to my face talking like I never did a darn thing

I run alone, don't have time to run with clique
Stayed to myself; that's why I worry about my own biz
That's why I don't mess with the paint
I don't hang around clowns
Do what I gotta do like the way that sounds
I'm getting older now
I continue to brush the dirt off my shoulders
I got a future ahead of me
Trying to lay down my plans
Ain't trying to let stuff backfire on me
It don't matter if I'm not liked before I get married
Trying to enjoy these days of my life
I say: nobody will tell me what to do
I decide my own life

By Trancy Custis AKA Tbone Snackz

Gotta Stay True To Myself

Got a lot of heat in my life already repeated once
Not trying to repeat it twice
So I'm sitting here sweating
You'd think I was a gambler the way I was at the casino betting
It's a hard life all by yourself
Somebody's got to live that's why I stay to myself
Yet I continue to lend a helping hand
Gotta stay in focus; can't change my plans now
Trying to live life better
As a young man I look back at my life when I was just a kid
You know you gotta keep it real
I'm a tell just how it is surviving
Taking care of my biz; my head's hurting
Stress and pains, just a lot of stuff in my life
Like I ain't got nothing to gain; my situation still ain't right

Still having bad dreams in my sleep at night
God please send me a sign or come and change my life

By: Trancy Custis AKA Tbone Snackz

Your Heart Was Broken Until I Came

Let's talk baby
Take a walk, baby
I see you looking lonely and stuff
Love wasn't right,
Broke your heart; that's got to be tough
I know how you feel
I'm going to keep it real
The pain inside of you is making you ill
Felt sorry for you, know it was hard for you
Girl, you gotta let it go now
Times are fast
You can't be slow
I'm what you need;
We can succeed
All you have to do is believe
"Cos we were meant to be
Just want to hold you and hug you in my arm
Like it's supposed to be
Keep walking up
You say things seem the same
Looking at you in the mirror you say you need to change
It's your life
You don't have to go through that pain
Come with me and be my queen; I can be your king
Look at me, I can change everything
Just want to be different

I'm not the same; I want to put a smile on your face
Telling you you're in the right place
Protecting you like it's supposed to be
Hold you tight and close to me
I'm your man that's how it's going to stand

By: Trancy Custis AKA Tbone Snackz

Help Me Out; I Need a Healing

Things have changed; whole situation is different
Now I've been by myself, didn't have no friends
Faced my own problems, my ups and downs
Nobody to talk to when my pain was around
Felt so bad; didn't even want to be here
There was no love for me
Like nobody even cared
All emotional and everything but I couldn't shed a tear
Sitting there asking God: why?
Going through this pain every year
Feeling down and everything
Tossing and turning at night; couldn't even sleep
Having crazy dreams about me leaving the world
I was just being real
Even thought about I grabbing a bottle of pills
I can't let these people take me outta here
I'm strong, so I gotta survive
Don't care who don't like me, still got my pride
Went through so much pain like I wanted to cry
Something's still missing but I don't know why
Couldn't walk a mile in my shoes even if you tried
It's hard for me to get stuff out 'cos I hold everything on the inside
Keep beating myself up, don't why
Trying to find answers so I'm looking the sky

Too many clouds in the way as I'm looking for my God
I'm sitting here praying for a change
"Cos I'm tired of going through all this pain

By: Trancy Custis AKA Tbone Snackz

I Need Saving

God; please wash away my pains
Tell me things aren't going to be the same
I just want you to give me hope
Tell me I don't have to pull on that rope
Tired of holding my head down
Help me to come back around
Feels like I'm up in the air
Just want to reach the ground
Take your hands and wipe away my tears
Tell me it there's still people out there that cares
I know what I've been through
But just keep me here; give me a sense of direction
Tell me everything is real
Just want my life to change; don't like it the way it is
Lord; just touch me with your hands
Make me a better man
Open up doors for me
Give me more to see
Tell me life is what you make it to be
Come down from heaven and save me
Just shine on me
You're my light; do these things for me
Change my life

By: Trancy Custis AKA Tbone Snackz

I've Been through A Lot

I'm Trancy Custis, no joke; people said I wouldn't make it but I always had hope
Been yanked around all my life, like someone was pulling on the rope; they said I was high like I was on dope
My life was drowning like someone threw me off the boat
Talk about me now but I'm okay
You haters hating now you'd better get out my way
I'm coming through; nothing about me you can't say
I'm still living proof doing things my way ain't for the ball
'Cos I don't play
Trying to live life day to day
A lot of y'all been testing me for years
You want me to flip
But in the back of my mind I don't care
Keep the fake people from around me; I'm too real
Minus the pain and the tears I'm going through
I see my life switching gears
Yea, I got a sickness that's making me ill
That's why I grab a bottle of those medication pills
Through it all I can say
I'm still here

By Trancy Custis AKA Tbone Snackz

I Came A Long Way But I Made It

Just sitting here; wondering what's going through my head
Can't go to sleep at night thinking about the stuff I've done said
Nobody can understand the life I done had
Try walking a mile in my shoes
But if you can't even do half just sit back with a straight face and don't even laugh
You can't experience what I been through

Put the shoes on the other foot
Imagine all the pain I went through
Talking with family; thought they would have my back
When it was time to ride I was by myself; family ain't jack
I still live my life as Tbone Snackz
They said in the real world you need friends
I'm still saying I don't need none of them
People used to tell me I would never make it on my own
I never looked back 'cos I stayed strong
Still living life don't see what I'm doing wrong
I don't have fears
I get emotional, yea I shed a tear
You keep talking about me I don't care
I'm walking with God now, I'm just being real
I used to be in park now I'm switching the gears
Yeah, I let people get under my skin
No, I'm not a loser; I was born to win
I know I wasn't living right
'Cos I chose to stray from the hood
Raised in the streets; devils were beating me up
Now it's time for satan's defeat
I'm standing here looking up at the sky
I raised both my hands in the air giving
My thanks to God

By Trancy Custis AKA Tbone Snackz

I Felt Like Giving Up But I Didn't!

All my life I been through a lot of tests
I wanted to give up 'cos it was nothing but stress
God didn't want me to leave;
He said: Hang in there, you're gonna be blessed
Cos He knew my life was a mess
When I used to go through problems

I would sit around and think:
I know I'm stronger than that. Why am I telling myself I can't?
Just felt sorry for myself
Picked up a bottle and started to drink
I'm asking God: why am I going through the pain?
The stuff I did in my life don't even feel the same
I'm so not right
Now I keep hearing someone calling my name
I'm going to find you I have to walk through
The storm and the rain
Keep telling myself I ain't supposed to be here
My life was supposed to end
Thank You Lord for a second chance
I'll find you again
The devil tried to get me
But in God's Presence I know I wasn't supposed to sin
Wasn't supposed to mark my body up
Got Tbone Snackz on my skin
I know it's something in my life that I haven't done right
Just wanna start over and
Have a new life
I'm just trying to have that bond and get closer to Christ

By Trancy Custis AKA Tbone Snackz

I've Got Love For My Mother

All things are possible
Without you mom I never would've made it
Nine months of pain you went through
We made it
You were a strong woman, I'm glad you knew how to take it
No matter what they say
You always stood by my side
You taught me to survive
You made it okay for me to cry

Yea, I admit I'm an emotional guy
The feelings that I have makes me feel good
You made it easy for me to pick my own friends
Told me don't lean on them too much
They won't be there for you in the end
'Till you find got someone good that's going to be there
That's who you call your friend
Taught me how to be independent 'cos I really don't
Need none of those not so good friends
Mom you're special 'cos you always cared
When I didn't have anybody, you were always there
Know I took you through a lot
The love I have for you is too deep
That will never stop
Tbone Snackz is the name
I'm going to rock
Know I'm hard headed and setting in my ways
Nobody's perfect you know
As long as I'm here you ain't gotta worry about living in fear
 Dial one number, your son is always going to be right here
Without you who knew where I would be
You gave me life I thank God for you
You took the time out your schedule for me
I ain't the best kid around
I'll always have love for you
Until they decide to put me in the ground
Got a smile on my face
Nobody can keep me down
Don't care about the haters, they hate on me now
What would this world be like if there wasn't no me?
I got love for my mother
Don't care what y'all believe

By Trancy Custis AKA TBone Snackz

I Gotta Let It Be Known

Just want someone that I can chill with
Know what they want in life and keep it real
Just want to live drama free
Gotta be cool and want to have fun
Just chill with me
Might be a different approach; still got the same swag
No fitted hats; only doo rags
My style is expensive, you can tell by the price tag
Just in a league of my own
Though I stay to myself, I'm in the zone
There's only one of me, so don't even try to clone
I done seen a lot of things with my own eyes
A lot of things done caught me by surprise
It's either you're with me or against me but
But I'm still gonna survive
Always been put in situations where I didn't belong
Seems like people are praying for me to take a fall
I'm telling them I can't, the games not over
'Cos I'm still holding my holding the ball
The clock is running, time is running out
In a jam; like I can't get out
Still holding my head up, you haters
Thought family had my back but I was wrong
I'm walking with God now; that's where I belong
Yeah, I can forget and forgive but the way my life was like
I couldn't live, even stopped me from seeing my own kids
Some things I thought weren't even real
You don't know my pain or how I feel

By Trancy Custis AKA Tbone Snackz

I Just Need To Change My Life

Just sitting here weighing out the options in my life
Talking about the good and the bad that happened in my Life
It's kind of hard to explain
This is some real stuff; can't you tell from the pain
Some situations got so tough, it's been a struggle
Every day was rough
As the years went by some things stayed the same
I'm lost like I have nothing to gain
I done seen it all
Standing up only to take a fall
People see me in the trouble just trying to make it
Fall down a couple times, gotta get up
That's the way it is
Tell me that I was a troubled kid
Been through a lot of stuff
Nobody else knows how rough my life was
You can look at me and tell I've been through a lot tears
Back in the day they tried to take my life
Thank the Lord for letting me see the light
It seems like everything is looking good
It hasn't been the same since living in the hood
You think you know me just because you know my name
Never been where I've been, can't even feel my pain
I'm still the same person
Praying to get a lot of stuff off my chest
I'm tired of going through all this stress
Need a different life; tired of this mess

By Trancy Custis AKA Tbone Snackz

I Need You BABY

I need you more than ever
I can't let you go and that means never
You and I are meant to be together
You got me so I can't say good bye
When I'm looking at you the tears run down my eyes
We got to make this thing last
That means we must survive
You make me smile when I'm around you
You complete my life glad I found you
When I had nothing you stuck by my side
Through it all; now that's something!
You're the realist
It ain't no frontin'
I feel it in my heart
You're the one baby
I love you 'cos you're the Number one woman to me
You mean the world to me
It ain't hard to see
I can't live life without you and me

By Trancy Custis AKA Tbone Snackz

I Want My Grand mom Back

I toss and turn in my sleep
Things cross my mind, it's just so deep
Seems like everything gets to me
I can't seem to let go of stuff in my life
I gotta know
Trying to keep a smile on my face
The pain inside of me I'm trying to erase
Some things I'm trying to forget

Want them to go away; why does it keep coming back
Feels like I'm losing my mind
God give me something; throw me signs
I'm tired of losing; just want to win some times
This is my life, tired of crying sick
Tired of all the lies
Why am I still wiping the tears?
Wish my grand mom was here
Why did she have to say goodbye
I don't feel right; I'm all crushed inside
I'm never going to give up
I'm always trying
Still asking myself: God why?
Sorry for all the things I did growing up
Just want her back
Make life the way it is supposed to be.

By Trancy Custis AKA Tbone Snackz

You Don't Know How I Feel

The feelings I have inside you'll never understand
You're trying to find a way out but it's hard
So I gotta let it go
Yo! I still find myself living in the past
I'm getting older now
Keep asking myself: how long will it last?
Still struggling in my finances, low on cash
You can look at me and tell
I hide feelings with a smile; who am I kidding?
Just a young kid who don't live in fear
Since nobody gave me respect, why should I care?
Growing up, it always seemed I was by myself
Didn't care who didn't like me as long as I had love for myself
being in a family I was always the black sheep

My feelings go way down inside, it's just too deep
My life is hurting from all the pain
People would say: don't worry, I'm always be on your side
Getting all emotional and stuff, tears rolling down my eyes
They bounced on me, caught me by surprise
Didn't know who I was anymore
Just a lot of pains and my body was sore
I see a different life ahead of me some things I gotta improve
You're looking at a changed dude
There's still stuff in my life I gotta do good

By Trancy Custis AKA Tbone Snackz

I Wouldn't Be Here; But Thanks be to GOD

This is the biggest blessing of my life
I'm on the road to some good things
I'm heading to some good things
Stuff like this: blowing out some candles
Waiting on a wish
Ain't nothing but good things
Nothing but happiness
I can live without the pain
I was stuck in park; couldn't go nowhere
But in my dreams feels like I've been everywhere
Like I was running away in my dreams
Things were rough
But it's not as hard as it seems
Jumping up out of my sleep
Asking myself: what's wrong with me?
Whatever I'm going through, God please cover me
Sitting here; don't want life to pass by
I owe all my success to You, God
That's why I'm holding my hands up to the sky

By Trancy Custis AKA Tbone Snackz

If It's Not Them, They Ain't Trying To Help

People ain't trying to help you when it's not them
That's why I don't hang around fake people
Don't care if it's my own kind; I do what I gotta do
Don't need none of them
Sometimes I just sit around and think: see who's real
Pointing out the ones that ain't
I was born by myself
Don't need friends
Never asking for anything
Had my own ends; why even bother
Nobody's trying to help
Everybody's worrying about themselves
Some people make me sick; all they do is talk
I can go anywhere as long as my two legs let me walk
You reap what you sow; telling you what I know
You know how it goes
Right now some are down and out
If you never been where we've been
Don't know what it's all about
Tough times, feeling trapped in the drought
We don't need nobody or do we?
Long as we got each other, know what it's like brother
People laughing at us like it's funny
Our blessings will come through; were going to get
That money

By Trancy Custis AKA Tbone Snackz

I'm Just Tired Of This Pain

When I think about all the pain I went through
Who knew where I would be today?
Thank God every day for setting me free
Faced a lot of problems in my life
Some things just were not right
It was a struggle each day, had to put up a fight
Going through pain was just making me weak
A lot of stuff made me ask: Why did this have to happen to me?
Time after time seemed like I cried my last tear
Did God bring me this far just leave me here?
Feels like I'm all alone, I don't understand
My life feels so weird
I'm stuck in park trying to switch the gears
Trying to overcome all the pain I felt for so many years
Give me guidance, just show me the way
Tell me everything is going to be okay
Give me a smile back
Tell me it's going to be a brighter day
Just want you to make me proud
I'm looking up in the sky
Hoping I don't ever see that black cloud
Been going through this ever since I was a small child
I'm looking at my life
Wishing mine would never have fallen apart
Sitting there thinking: Why did they have to break my heart?
 I'm sick of this pain
Tired of crying
Was going to give up
But I'll keep on trying
I'm on both of my knees praying for a better life
God please make everything right

By Tracy Curtis AKA Tbone Snackz

I'm Just Trying To Make It

I'm in the sky, a shining dog
Every day of my life is a struggle
That's why I'm a keep trying
Y'all always see me doing different stuff
This is my life, like I haven't already done enough
I came a long way holding my head up
I still wish for a better life
Trying to make everything right
I know what tough times are all about
Drink occasionally when I'm feeling stressed
But I'm still looking at myself everyday in the mirror
Thinking about what I can do different
Used to hate my life, playing the blame game
I'm still the same person playing the same game
Hurting right now, gotta a lot of pain
Stay out of my way; stay in your own lane
Trancy Custis is the birth name
If you don't know me I'm real friendly
Had a lot of problems
Made me some enemies
It seems life goes round and round
Like I'm in a circle
Tired of losing, gotta win
I bruise easy from the marks on my skin
You talk about good but I'm living the bad
Going through life without seeing my real Dad
Every day I see the same ol' thing
Tired of going through life with stress and pain

By: Trancy Custis AKA Tbone Snackz

I'm Just Waiting On My Blessing

I'm in a tough situation; time is running against me
I got the patience
People don't care when it's not their situation
All out of options, ain't nothing left
Trying to lend a helping hand, with some worrying only about themselves
Laughing and joking like it's a game
What they don't know is I'm in a lot of pain
I got a family to protect; that will never change
Struggling to find money to get something to eat
Trying to keep a roof over our heads so we don't end up in the streets
Just thinking about it my heart paces fast beat
Staying up a real late, can't even sleep
Shaking knees, getting no help
I don't know what to do anymore
We're out for ourselves
Hate when people say your situation's not theirs
Experiencing the pain
Tears in my eyes, it hurts so much
I can't even cry
Holding all my feelings on the inside
Why did this have to happen to us?
I'm asking God: why just sitting here praying for a blessing?
I'm losing my head right now 'cos all I'm doing is stressing
Got to hold my head up and be strong
Don't tell me everything's going to be alright 'cos you may be wrong
I'm just waiting
God's gonna put us where we belong

By Trancy Custis AKA Tbone Snackz

I'm Still Looking For You

Sitting here looking at my grandma's picture
Wondering why you ain't in my picture
Tears running down my face
Trying to put you back in that place
Why did you have to leave my life?
What did you do to deserve this? It ain't right
Like somebody stabbed me in my heart with a knife
I wish you were still here so I wouldn't have to shed more tears
Everything was so clear with you
You're gone now but I still feel that you're near
It's so hard losing someone you love
I'm still reaching out to from above
You're gone and it's hard to see
I know you're in heaven waiting for me

By Trancy Custis AKA Tbone Snackz

I'm Thankful For Being Here

I want to thank y'all for being here for me
Listen; when I was growing up I only wanted to be free
You gave me the tools to build my life
I just wanted everything to go right
You taught me to become a good man in life
You made me feel better when I was going through
You supported me in my decisions
You taught me something new everyday
You held my hand along the way
Encouraged me to follow my dreams
Wiped my tears when I was feeling sad
Thank you for being there, Mom and Dad
You calmed me down when I got mad

If I never knew what I had I might lose everything
Each day might be your last
Life is what you make of it
You steered me in the right direction so I had to take it

By Trancy Custis AKA Tbone Snackz

It Hurts Me My Family Gotta Live Like This

I can't even focus; a lot's on my mind
That's why my eyes stay open
I hold everything in the inside
It's causing me a lot of pain
Done lost everything, whole situation done changed
I point fingers at myself 'cos I'm part of the blame
Only thing I got left is my name
It's up to me to carry the weight on my shoulders
Tossing and turning and rolling over
I done seen my life flash before my eyes; thought it was over
I got a family to protect, how can I?
When you lose it there ain't nothing left
Trying to survive off a little bit of money in my check
Like life's a mess, I'm just trying to make it; it's bringing on stress
They said you need eight hours sleep; I must not be getting proper rest
Heard people say it will get better
How can it, staying in a hotel week to week, eating a lot of cheddar?
Put your feet in my shoes, you'll never understand unless you been there
You can't understand my pain
Man; got my family into this situation, gotta get out of a jam

Put the pieces to the puzzle back together and come up with a plan
It's hard up here in the streets if you know what I'm saying
That's why I hold my hands together
Al I'm doing is praying
Just gotta keep my head up and stay strong
It's hard to do right when everything else seems wrong

By Trancy Custis AKA Tbone Snackz

Just Felt 'COS

Didn't know who I was anymore
'Cos a lot of things I went through was my fault
Just sitting alone thinking about the stuff I have done
Came too far in life for people to tell me I can't
Thought my life was over but it just begun
Nobody was treating me right, not even my own mother
I was her son
Just wanted my life to be over
Why am I going through this; GOD let my pain be over
Couldn't even hang around anyone
I was just too sad and always held a frown
Couldn't even laugh
One day I'm going to be pain free
Got to forget the bad memories
You don't know that it's like being me
Used to tell my family my problems but they didn't care
Life was hard 'cos nobody was there
Still having dreams, waking up at night
Seemed like my world was coming to an end
Nobody to share it with, didn't even have a friend
I went through life though I paid the cost
Tell me what I need to know tired of being 'cos

By Trancy Custis AKA Tbone Snackz

Just Going Through Something

Got my thoughts together so I stay focused
Gotta see everything
That's why my eyes stay open
I'm trying to be careful about everything I do in life
Listening to other people and taking in advice
There's a lot of stuff in this world so you gotta know what you want
One life to live; all I do now is sit and chill
What's the deal?
You know me, I keep it real
Always trying to keep my head up, gotta stay strong
I talk about life in all of my poems
History it talking
Nobody showed me the way to write
Had to teach myself
I was born a winner so I can't lose
Stay to myself, that's what I know
Don't care what you think, I gotta remain cool
Take the pain out of my body so I can be free
Tired of crying, wipe away my tears
Tired of the life I have, let me switch the gears
Have respect for everybody including my peers
Thought my pain was going to take me out
Felt like giving up 'cos I didn't care
God carried me along way that's why I'm still here….

By Trancy Custis AKA Tbone Snackz

Living Life

I just want to focus on myself and do my own thing
Tired of going through life with headaches and pains
Learning how to walk on my own

Do I need somebody to hold my hand?
I make my own choices; decisions all mine
I'm a grown man
Thank those who helped me in my times of need
For the ones that don't know me just call me Tee
I'm a keep my head up and just believe in me
Used to have everything going my way
Now it's kind a hard 'cos I'm struggling everyday
You got to learn from your mistakes
Ain't feeling good these days, body starting to ache
Hoped raining days would wash away my pain
Just gotta put my thoughts together and use my brain
Tired of doing the same ol thing
Never had much help
I'm seeing my way, put me down all you want
I might be down but I'm not gone
'Cos life is all about experiences ……

By: Trancy Custis AKA Tbone Snackz

LORD, Come And Wipe My Pain Away

I closed my eyes
But I could still see
What was happening to me?
Telling myself this can't be
Come on God, set me free
Still find myself going through a phase
I'm in and out it like I'm going through a maze
Just trying to see some better days
Trying to enjoy life without things getting in my way
Here I am looking back at time
Taking these steps
This life is mine
Looking at life trying to figure out where I stand

Got choices in both of my hands
Going through life it was tough
Every situation I faced seemed like it get rough
Tears falling like rain
I was trying to do hide my pain
It was like it never healed
You can't imagine how I feel
Wishing my grandfather was still here
Everything I feel is not counted for
Felt like I just can't do anything right
I need help, that's why I call on the name of the Lord God

By Trancy Cuslis AKA Tbone Snackz

LORD: Give ME A Sign

People keep on eyeing, I'm like what did I do?
They tried to get the best of me but I'm no fool
Just a different swag and a different attitude
Don't try to give me a bad rap
I don't fool with you
Been the black sheep, what's up with that?
Always been a leader no matter what
Never following in nobody's foot steps
So I sit here and wonder
Is that how I got myself into a jam?
Put a lot of pressure on my health
Choose the right path of life
'Cos don't want it to end up in the wrong hands
I want to do something different
That's why I'm praying for a change
People still speaking my name
I'm a do me
One thing about it I can't change
Never was the one to hold any grudge
All I was looking for was nothing but love
Turn my life around, Lord

Give me luck
Feels like I'm still stuck ….

By Trancy Custis AKA Tbone Snackz

Living Life Until the End

My life still rough
Seems like yesterday everything happened
Stuff still messed up
You couldn't walk a mile in my shoes
Even if I told you, you would be all confused
Pain running through my body like I got abused
Had many problems
I would just talk to old heads while we were in the back yard throwing horse shoes
I'm a winner so I can't lose
Don't owe anybody nothing, what else to do?
I got to improve
You can always catch people hating, they might be your friend or some kind of relation
I don't like negative things so don't bring them to my face
I mind my own business, I stay in my place
Let me talk about the facts all these years
Growing up had to watch my own back
Trying to smile in my face then wanting me to cut you slack
I love life, still having fun
Out of all my mom's kids I'm her only son
You can look into my eyes and see my pain
I done cast everything like I don't have anything to gain
I'm letting everything ride
I knew how to deal with stuff that's why I always survived
Best thing about it; still kept my pride
I'm Trancy Custis; I feel good inside

By Trancy Custis AKA Tbone Snackz

My Life's All Messed Up

I'm sitting here just waiting on my blessing
Situation getting badder, so that means I'm still stressing
Been through the ups and downs; can't smile, all I do now is frown
I'm a do what I gotta do for my family and continue to hold things down
The way I see it everybody's the same
My attitude's changed
I'm a totally different guy still having dreams in my sleep
About going to die
Had nowhere to go
Turned to my family, didn't get any help
The only person I had was God
Sleeping in my car on a cold night
Weighing all of the options, situation wasn't even right
A lot on my mind, wondering what to do next
Take one day at a time and continue with my steps
My life's gonna change, put ya money up
That's a bet on my life
I been going through pain
Tired of people playing me, like I'm a game
Driving me crazy like I'm going insane
Tbone Snackz until I die; that's a sure thing
I don't care about feelings, I've been doing me
Was in such stress it was like a maze
See myself enjoying some better days
You can't tell me what to do anymore
Doing everything my way
You think you know me because you know my name
You ain't never been where I've been
Can't understood my pain

By Trancy Custis AKA Tbone Snackz

My One And Only Friend

I thought you were my friend even called you my homeboy
The things I tried to talk to you about you were trying to avoid
We were closer than ever, we were like brothers
We belonged together; had each other's back
As kids I can't even believe some of the stuff you did told me
You said to stay out of your face and mind my biz
I was trying to help you
What did I do to deserve this?
Always been by your side
Through thick and thin we always survived
Me and you not being friends anymore hurt inside
I never gave up on you, always been your friend
You're my riding partner; we're going to ride until the end
Let's put everything behind us and be friends again
Whatever we're going through, let's leave it in the past
I like the good times, we shared a good laugh
You're my friend! that will always be
Friendship forever; yes indeed!

By Trancy Custis AKA Tbone Snackz

No Hope, Felt Like Giving Up

Lord, why am I not getting treated fair?
I tried to be nice, but it's got no respect in here
People go out their way calling out ya name
Pointing fingers at me and telling everybody that I'm the blame
The best way I'm going to leave is pain free, with no stress;
Everything's behind me, ready to lay down and rest
My body's hurting like I ain't got no strength left
Every day of my life I been put to the test
Still standing here telling you I'm blessed

Good things coming
Twenty eight years now, still counting the dates
Still living life the way it is
I'm focused on myself, worrying about my own biz
I've been doing me, what else can I say?
As long as I'm happy at the end of the day
It's just your ordinary chess player
Gotta move on with life, can't continue to play chess
You just gotta take me for who I am
Don't judge me 'cos God is the only one
Who really knows who I am

By Trancy Custis AKA Tbone Snackz

No One Knows Me Better Than GOD

The life I'm living don't even seem right
It's like everywhere I gotta put up a fight
What have I done to people for me not to be liked?
Feel like I'm all alone
Don't care what the haters say about me I'm still in the zone
They tried to take me out but I'm where I belong
You sit back and watch a lot of things
Where I came from some things didn't even change
I remember everything, still carrying some of the pain
Some people were praying for me to leave this place
I almost did from all the problems I faced
Most times I would drop to my knees
Get in a corner thinking about all the stuff I've been through
Asking God: why this had to happen to me?
He said: Don't give up just yet
Waiting patiently on my day to shine
I'm still looking at my clock waiting on my time
I've been through a lot of stuff I'm tired of crying
Lord, nobody understands me but You

They don't know all the pain I went through

By Trancy Custis AKA Tbone Snackz

Only The Strong Shall Survive

The world's getting crazy now
Family and friends done walked on me
I'm fine 'cos I remember everything my grand mom told me
You got some real friends, then you got some fake friends
If you know what I'm talking about then you can relate
Man, I'm looking at life chasing it full speed
Turning upside down catching nothing but a nose bleed
Say anything you want about me
Don't care what y'all think
Forget you and your next to kin
Tbone Snackz got that labeled in my skin
Been having crazy dreams about me being rich
When I'm going through my problems just grabbed the bottle
Somebody got me trapped in the corner
Gave up a lot of blood but I'm not no donor
All I do is relax and chill
Keep the fake people from around me if you know how I feel
Never forget the name Tbone Snackz
Somebody should know there hasn't been nobody like me
As real as I am

By Trancy Custis AKA Tbone Snackz

Trying To Enjoy Myself

I'm Trancy Custis; what to do?
Trying to figure out my every move
You don't have a clue

Still wondering, all confused
You know me, I'm the same dude
Head was all messed up like I'm missing a few screws
People pushing me now, wanting me to flip
Can't let them get to me, got to get a grip
I remember when I used to sit and chill
Listening to people on how they kept it real
No fake people around, that's how I feel it
Ain't no competing
Body and life all messed up, like I took a beating
I'm a winner
Friends you knew for years turned their backs on you
Spit and said my situation wouldn't change
God, help me go through this stress
I got no strength left
Something good is going to come out of this
And that's a bet!

By Trancy Custis AKA Tbone Snackz

FAMILY

You're the one for me

Loving you is the best thing I ever did
I accepted you into my heart and your kids
Who knew one day we would become husband and wife
By putting this ring on your finger
That's one thing that I like; we're committed to each other
God wanted us together for life
In the beginning our situation was a mess
But we got through our tough times
I guess it was a lot of tests
I found my queen
You've been praying for a good man and I'm your king
I'm a take care of you for life and that's a sure thing
I'm here to make you happy, not to because you pain
I'm here for you and you're here for me
Nobody else you would rather have that's better than me
God threw you signs; it's not hard to see
My love for you is deep and that's my promise for life
I'm so happy that you're going to
Be my wife

By Trancy Custis AKA Tbone Snackz

The Love Of My Life

I'm so crazy; what do you think of me, baby?
Just confused a little bit
The man of dreams; that must be it
Trying to figure: what do I want?
A nice lady who won't put on a front
I just want to take long walks
Conversation that lasts for a while
Just want to chill with you

Trust what I'm saying and keep it real
Want to keep a smile on your face
Want you to be happy knowing you're in the right place
Let's go to a nice movie, sit down and have a quiet dinner
You ain't with no loser; you're riding with a winner
I know how to treat a lady, I ain't no beginner
Just want to hold you close to my heart
Seen something special in you from the start
You can tell your friends about me: this guy's special
He's the one for me
I ain't telling y'all no lies; I must be the one for you
Girl, I see it in your eyes, I'm always a gentleman
Everywhere we go you're mine and I'm yours
Ain't gotta put on a show
Just want you to be my beau
Want to be happy and spend life with you
I've seen a smile on your face every time I came through
You didn't even know what to do
You were a standout chick so I chased you
Imagine what other people are saying about you
We're going to be together and that's a fact
I love you with all my heart and that's that

By Trancy Custis AKA Tbone Snackz

One Year ANNIVERSARY

Our first year together has been nothing but great
Being married to you makes everything right
You're special to me, brought joy to my life
I thank God for sending you to me and making you my wife
I'm so happy we're a couple and the things we do
The day we got married when you said "I do"
I didn't know love could be true
By putting this ring on your finger we wed

We're together forever
That means in life we're perfect for each other
That's gotta be right
You're the one for me
You're the love of my life

By Trancy Custis AKA Tbone Snackz

MOM, You're SPECIAL

Mom I want to thank you for everything you've done
I'm so proud that I'm your son
In most cases you stuck by my side
Taught me to hope so I kept it by my side
I'm strong today, told you I can survive
It's okay for you to cry, I know it hurts you inside
Always around to say the right things
Even when I was going through my pain
Told me my situation would change
I kept beating myself up saying: I'm the blame
Some things didn't feel the same
Mom, you are special to me
You're great, yes indeed
You mean the world to me
Sometimes I can't express the love I have for you
I'm writing this just for you
Forgive me for all the times I made you mad
Sorry I took you through all the problems I had
You gave me some good advice and you made me laugh
Where would I be if you were never here?
Mom, I love you; showing you I care

By Trancy Custis AKA Tbone Snackz

You're My Son

What makes you a great, son?
It's the stuff you do and the things you've done
You might not be my birth child but having you in my life brings a smile
I just want to play with you
Spend the whole day with you
You just want someone like me
Without you in my life, where would I be?
Looking at you, it's like when I was young
I miss that age growing up and having fun
You're a good kid, I'm glad that you're my son
Wish I could take back all the bad things I have done
Don't be hard headed like I was
How rough did it get!
I always used to get in my little ways
Even when my parents told me to behave
I just had to break the rules
Why didn't I do what I was told?
You grow up really fast, just looking back at my past
You're the son I've been waiting for
You're here at last

By Trancy Custis AKA Tbone Snackz

You're All That I Need

You're my favorite girl; want you to know that
You're happy to do whatever I liked
You even showed that even when the situation got rough
You were there to show me love
Where I would be without you?
You've been there since day one

I knew our love was true
I wasn't always the best guy
Even looked you in the face and told you a lie
I thought we were going to end but we showed everybody how the strong do survive
I treated you so bad, seen the tears forming in your eyes
I knew we were meant for each other
And never once did we say our goodbyes
I know that I was in the right place 'cos I was sent there by God
You complete me; you're all right
I'm here for you and you're here for me
Tbone Snackz is your heart
It ain't hard to see I'm a be your husband
You're gonna be my wifey
I'm a treat you like a fresh pair of Nike's
That means I'm a take care of you inside and out
You're the love of my life; no doubt!

By Trancy Custis AKA Tbone Snackz

You Mean Everything To Me

Your hair blows like the wind
You're my everything; my affection
The smile on your face lights up a whole room
You're like a pretty little flower just waiting to bloom
When I look into your eyes
I see we were meant for each other
We can't say our goodbyes
The love we have for one another since the very start
It must have been something special 'cos you're my heart
Year after year we get stronger
You're like my stomach when I don't eat
You're my hunger
The skin on your body is so soft

Holding you in my arms at night
Listening to you talk
The way you hold your head slightly against my chest
I knew you were the one
You're the best love of my life
It don't get no better than that it is
It's easy to express the way I feel
'Cos my love for you is real

By Trancy Custis AKA Tbone Snackz

Can't Let You Go

If love is blind why can I still see?
Now I must be the man 'cos I'm in your town
I was born a loser
So love stays in my heart
I'm just your average dude
Candy flowers, whatever you want, I'll cater to you
Let's go somewhere nice and quiet
Have a candle light dinner in this little room
Want to make sure you're comfortable and the mood is right
You're not going nowhere
We're going to be here all night
Rose pedals in the bed
And all that soapy bath water is where we're going to relax
Trying to take your mind off all the bad that happen in your life
Just want us to cuddle together
So we can hold each other at night wrap
You up in my arms like you supposed to be
Hold you real close to me
I'll change your whole life and make everything right

By Trancy Custis AKA Tbone Snackz

I'm Happy

Happy times comes, then it goes
No one knows but you
What you're happy for
Might be for the good or the bad
Smiling one minute, then it turn right
Said; how long will it last?
Good friends that stick by your side
Those are the ones you wish you had
Thought I had good luck but it turn into the bad
What I'm looking for I never had had
Enough, enough! I'm looking for more
I've turned my frowns into smiles
That's how it used to be when I was a small child
What may seem to make you weak only makes you stronger
My grandparents told me joy comes in the morning
You've just got to hold on and keep your head
It won't take that long
I'm happy
That's where I belong

By Trancy Custis AKA Tbone Snackz

I Just want you to be Happy

I want a happy everything kiss
Hug me, love me; you're the rays of sunshine in my life
I'll do whatever you need, don't care about the price
You're my world; I'm trying to make everything right
You bring a smile to my face
My love for you can't be erased
I must be the one 'cos I was put into that place
To share all the good times
I'm there to wipe the tears from your eyes

You're the light of my world; the best thing that ever happen to me
Even when you're feeling all weak
Lay your head against my chest, listen to my heart beat
I can't live life without you and me
Being happy that's where I wanna be
Turn all your frowns into smiles
Let you lay in my arms for awhile
Let you know you're always going to be safe
I'll put a big grin on your face
Knowing that you're in the right place

By Trancy Custis AKA Tbone Snackz

Enjoy Your Life; Have Fun

Sitting here thinking: why wasn't my life all that great?
Live life to the fullest, that's what grand mom said
Don't let the little things get you down
Gotta live everyday
Run into problems, life was like a crash
Sometimes things go by really slow
Other times things go by fast
You can't take nothing for granted
I was stuck in park, like I was stranded
If this is my last day on earth accept my life for what it was worth
Always remember God is first
That goes for the young and the old and that's what I was told
Just have fun, enjoy life today
Never regret another day

By Trancy Custis AKA Tbone Snackz

Tired of Being Alone

I used to sit there all alone in an empty home
Starring off into the light
And thinking nobody's here with me, it's going to be a lonely night
I was blind; there was nothing for me to see
Can't be stuck here, there's got to be some place else
I got tired of living alone like this
Just need somebody to hold me
Felt like it was getting darker and the lights are starting to dim
Turning and looking, ain't nobody in sight
Telling God this can't be right
Send me someone to complete my life
This has got to be a dream
Just got to wake up
My heart was like it was going to break
All out of options, running out of time
Just want somebody I can call mine
Please send that person to my home
'Cos I'm tired of being all alone

By Trancy Custis AKA Tbone Snackz

The Thought of You Not Being Here

Since you been gone can't even catch a break
Opening my eyes to see you when I awake
You helped me with so much
Even with all the decisions I had to make
You were always there
Now I love but you're gone
I'm not used to this but not I'm all alone
In the time we spent together I never thought we would part
You're still there; you'll always be in my heart

You don't give up, do what you got to do
Every now and then I keep looking up
I know you're there 'cos I can feel the love
What I miss the most is our long talks
When things would bother me we would take long walks
Looking in the clouds; hoping to see your face again
You're the only one that could make me grin
But since you're gone it's like I have nothing left
The only person I have now is myself

By Trancy Custis AKA Tbone Snackz

You're a Good Friend

I been through a lot of hard times
My life didn't even seem fair
But through it all you were always there
Seems like you're always by my side to hold my hand
When I'm going through my problems you always understand
When I was weak you seemed to catch my feet
Couldn't get love at home
Had to get it in the streets
I'm grateful for the times we shared
You're a good listener I'm glad you cared
You're my true friend we've been here and there
You always had my back when I was against the wall
Told me to keep going
When I fell you rode with me until the end
I'm glad you a true friend

By Trancy Custis AKA Tbone Snackz

Missing You

I'm missing you Grandma, I'm so sad
Didn't know this pain could last
I'm still shedding tears; the thought of you not being here feels so weird
I just want you back; how long can the pain last?
Can't sleep at night thinking of you
Want to see your face, make my dreams come true
You're not here; what am I supposed to do?
Want to feel your touch and your love
Miss your kisses and hugs
You not being here ain't the same
Come back and take away my pain
We used to have talks, you taught me about life
Told me what I wasn't doing right
If I had any problems I would come to you
I still hear your voice; I'm missing you

By Trancy Custis AKA Tbone Snackz

When I Met You

The first time I met you I knew you were the one
Smile on your face, let's have some fun
Came and scooped you up, that was day one
Trying to get to know you nice and slow
Trying to make you my girlfriend
You know how that goes
Treat you like a queen, that's my motto
Me and you riding up and down the streets
I must be feeling you
Both of us enjoying ourselves, laid back in the seats
Finally I found a girl who was in love with me
Just sitting here trying to enjoy my night

Making sure that the situation is right
I got you, that's all that matters
Ain't got to chase nobody no more
No one else to chase after
You're the love of my life
And nobody can stop me; you're going to be my wife
It won't be long you'll have your ring
I'm your king, you're my world
You mean everything

By Trancy Custis AKA Tbone Snackz

A Loving Father

Sitting awake at night
Wondering would things ever be right
I lost my sight just to be like you
You're special to me; you're my daddy
Covered me with all your love
Not once did you ever hate me
Accepted who I was
You would take me
Showing me that you cared
Wasn't ashamed of me
You took me everywhere
You're the best that a son could ever have
Putting smiles on my face
Glad you're my dad
Cracked a joke here and there
Knew how to make me laugh
Going through life year after year
Thought you would leave my side
But you stayed right there
You protected me so I wouldn't have to live in fear

You're not only my dad, you're my provider
I didn't leave you either
I stayed right beside you
Me and you having talks about life
You've got to make the best of any situation
That's just life
I want to thank you for being My Dad
Without your guidance some things I would never have
A father and son bond can't be broken
It's because of you I got hope

By Trancy Custis AKA Tbone Snackz

Daddy's Baby Girl

I was busy each and every day
Didn't take the time out my life to even play
Daddy loves you in every way
Sometimes I get ahead of myself
I got to clean and cook
Forgot to read you a story in your book
You gave me that look
Even as I tucked you under the covers
You were afraid of the dark
I left on the night light
Checked on you, peeped through the door
Wish I could have done more
Had to lay down
I couldn't go to sleep and wondering why
In the middle of the night I heard you cry
Got up to see what was wrong
You were dreaming
It's okay baby, go back to sleep
Daddy's always going to be here
I ain't going nowhere

I love you - It's in my heart here
To put a smile on your face
Been like that from the start

By Trancy Custis AKA Tbone Snackz

Letting Go of the Past

I done been through a lot in my life
Felt like I didn't belong
Don't know what to do
Just got to stay strong
Didn't feel the same trying to overcome all my pain
Got caught up in my feelings
Telling myself I can't cry
Life is hard but I got to try
A lot of decisions I made was just so wrong
I got to keep my head band and stay strong
Taking one day at a time
Keep holding onto God
Why can't you hear my pain?
This is all I ask: please help me again
I'm dealing with real problems, it's not a game
A step closer to You, Lord is what was I thinking
What you do in life is always uncertain
This is my life I'm about to close the curtain
Change is coming
Tired of hurting

By Trancy Custis AKA Tbone Snackz

You're The Love of My Life

Baby, I love you with all my heart
Me and you forever; nobody can tear us apart
You make me feel good on the inside
You're that one chick so you know how to ride
You keep me happy; you know how you make me smile
Keep doing what you're doing, stay on the job
Never leave me or forsake me
Accept me the way I am that's the way you gotta take me
And never steer me in the wrong direction
Give me all your love and affection
Say it for me girl: Tbone Snackz is your blessing
I must be your heart because I hold the key
Can't say you without saying me
We were meant for each other, can't you see
At first it seem like you were blind
God even threw my name around, He even threw you signs
Me loving you; that's all the time
You're my gas pedal to my speed
You're my heart indeed
I can't spend life without you and me

By Trancy Custis AKA Tbone Snackz

Love For My Sisters

The love I have for my sisters nobody can take
They were there for me through my toughest break
Although it seems like were at each other throats
It's a bond that's stronger than ever; it can't be broke
We were always there for one another, no matter what
I'm their only brother
Always been stuck together

Can't break us apart
They mean the world to me; they're always in my heart
I got to protect them from a lot of hurt
That's my job, put that on every word
Sometimes I feel like they're not always there
They don't come around me like they don't even care
Yet all through my life y'all been right there
To share the smiles and the tears
The love I have for my sisters it will never end
They're more than that to me
They're my best friends

By Trancy Custis AKA Tbone Snackz

I Just Want You

I like you and only you; I don't care about the things you do
It's not about the clothes you wear or about the way that you do your hair
Or what kind of shoes you wear
I love you for you
Your skin is just so right; your eyes shine like a light
I'm glad that you're in my life
Want to know what makes you mad and what makes you sad
Just want to say the right things so I can see you laugh
I want to hold you close to my heart
Never want me and you to part
Want to know what you feel and that everything you know is real
Just want to hold you at night
Give you comfort and let you know things are right
'Cos it's you that I like; me and you forever
Now let's share life....

By Tracy Curtis AKA Tbone Snackz

PRAYERS

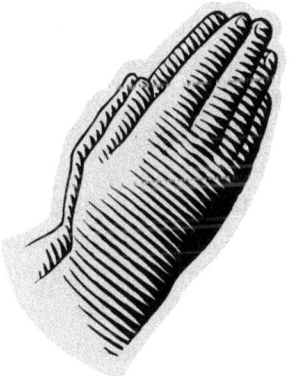

You've Gotta Love God and Others

Love is something that I got to do
If you don't love God you can't love the ones around you
I got love for myself and others
Can't forget about my sisters
And the one who made me who I am today, my mother
She showed me the finer things in life and taught me about life
That Man who died on the cross for our sins was Jesus Christ
Sometimes in life you've got to make a sacrifice
The road was hard for me getting past the devil
But mow I'm ahead in life
At first I didn't know anything
What "love"?
Yea, I was confused; things were rough
Turned to God for help and told Him I was stuck
Then it came to my mind that God is love
I thank the Lord everyday for my life
Blessing me with some beautiful kids and a wife
He gave up His only son so we can have a life
Don't have pain any more
I sleep peacefully at night
Love my Lord and Savior Jesus Christ

By Trancy Custis AKA Tbone Snackz

Trying to Feel Good Inside

This is my life, I'm a live it the way I want to live it
People pointing fingers at me
Everybody says don't try to get over it
But I'm not no fool
Seems like every time I try to be nice
Something I did in my life wasn't right
It's time for me to focus on big and better things
Had some real sick times and a lot of pain
Feels like nothing even changed
What is this life made out to be?
I'm hurting, can't you see I'm just trying to get rid of my pain?
Looking forward to the future
Seen some great things
My situation don't feel right
Always hold your head up, never let someone put you down
I'm stronger than that
Always got a smile never hold a frown
Do what I gotta do to hold my family down
Couldn't get my rest, a lot of things on my chest
Got to let it out now then I can feel at my best

By Trancy Custis AKA Tbone Snackz

Why is My Life So Messed Up?

I done seen everything in my life
Seen a lot of deaths so you know stuff haven't been right
My life is rough you already know
When I was a youngin' used to get teased
I wasn't feeling myself, this can't be me
God's the only one I trust
That's why I'm on both of my knees
I'm in this world by myself until the end

When you got money that's when you got friends
Yea I might not be big now, all my life I took all the put downs
Sooner or later I'll be laughing talking about: look at me now!
Ain't asking nobody for nothing
I'm grown now, don't need no help
I do everything on my own now
A lot of people of acting crazy
I don't care, your boy still amazing
I ain't the fastest dude but I'm watching my steps
God's the only one that will take my breath
Until then your boy is still going to be breathing
Got a lot of poems under my belt, all you gotta do is read them
I'm be chillin' every day and every night
You might know me but you don't understand my life

By Trancy Custis AKA Tbone Snackz

I Just want to be Happy

How do you know you're happy?
How can you tell your life is right?
I never can tell, my heart's hurting
I guess it's from the pain
My head's not right like I'm going insane
Like somebody's trying to pick apart my brain
Wash away all my problems when it rains
Still got my pride, still wiping the tears from my eyes
Still hurt on the inside
Still emotional like I want to cry
Still having talks with God
I want to be happy in every way
I'm still counting all the days
Just give me peaceful nights
Tell me everything going to alright
I know it will 'cos my future's bright

Give me good sight so I can see tell me this happiness is just for me
Whatever I'm going through
Set me free...

By Trancy Custis AKA Tbone Snackz

Just want my Pain to go Away

I'm standing outside with my shades on trying to hide my eyes
Can't take them off like I got a dark side
Stay cool in case somebody tries to walk
By lifting my hands up to the sky looking through the clouds
Can I see God? I want to ask Him:
Where should I be? I need your angels to carry me
I just don't feel right, there's no hope
Felt like giving up, can't do this any more
How long can this last?
My life is nothing, feels like trash I'm a keep pushing
It's going to be a drag but I can do anything
This is me, I'm a strong person; God, can't You see?
Just waiting on my life to change; trying to get rid of all my pain
He made me strong why can't I see?
I gotta be strong for everyone around me
Take my hand and never let it go
Teach me the things I need to know
Some people look at you really strange
I've got a great future ahead of me so I got everything to gain
It's hard for me to see past my pain
Seems like I went through a lot of stress and fears
Like the same thing repeats every year
Seems nothing got better, it just got worst
You can't feel what I feel if you've never been hurt

By Trancy Custis AKA Tbone Snackz

Thank You For Being There My Friend

In the real world you got some friends
I want to thank you for being there for me
This comes from a person who's been around for a while
In all my hard times you've been there
Seems like I have a lot of hate and fear in my eyes
'Cos there are so many things I don't understand
You wonder why I got my hands together
I'm praying for a better life, hoping everything will be alright
Was getting talked about like there was no respect
You always told me: God takes you through a series of tests
You always taught me how to be a young man
In the spirit of helping others out you always gave me a hand
Thank you for always being in my life
You gave me encouragement, gave me the best advice
I wouldn't be where I'm at if it wasn't for you
It was your words that made my dreams come true

By Trancy Custis AKA Tbone Snackz

Thank You for Caring

I just wanna say thank you for always being by my side
You taught me how to survive
Wiped my tears when I started to cry
Even when I was feeling bad on the inside
I never thought I would be the same young man
Ran away from my problems when I was in a jam
You were right there to always hold my hand even when I was feeling weak
This ain't the person I was made out to be
There were some things in life I couldn't see
Could not figure out where life would take me
I was lost and couldn't find my way

Going through pain you told me: everything will be okay
I told myself: gotta stay strong and hold my head
Until that day comes along you can hurt me but you can't take my pride
I'm a stay blessed 'cos I've got God on my side
With Him I'm always healed, no one else knows how I feel
I was going through life like I didn't care
But through it all I'm still here

By Trancy Custis AKA Tbone Snackz

The Road Wasn't Easy

Take a good look at my face I ain't scared
No tears in my eyes, walking with no fear
Keep asking myself: why am I still here?
I've witnessed a lot of stuff with my own eyes
Seen a lot of killings and drive bys
Growing up was a tough ol' life
Living in my hood wasn't nothing nice
You never put your guard down, never knew when you gotta fight
Who knew where I would be?
Could have been gone
Telling you I started at the bottom but now I'm on the top trying to figure out what I got?
You know me I still chill
I only hang out with the ones that keep it real
Don't care how y'all feel
I'm holding everything together so that means I'm still strong
Still by myself
Feel all alone; trying to figure why I don't belong
I had problems my whole life
Thought I could correct the situation
But stuff still ain't right

Got a lot of stuff on my chest 'cos it was really heavy
Thinking of things to keep me on board
The Lord knows my pain, how much more can I take before I break?
In my life I made a lot of mistakes
All I was looking for was help
Didn't find any; only had myself

By Trancy Custis AKA Tbone Snackz

Your Mind Can't Let You Go

I have no life; just like you left me
Take me for who I am; just accept me
I can't let you get away
I'm begging you, please stay
Can't see life without me and you
My love for you is true
If you leave me, what am I supposed to do?
I go crazy every time I hear your name
Just don't leave me or you'll take me through a lot of pain
I can't let you slip away, you're mine forever
That's what your voice said
Can't let you leave got a deep cut in my heart
Like I'm going to bleed
We need each other, you and me
Don't make me shed a tear
Spending life by myself knowing you're not here
I can't let you go
Know you're the love of my life
Come on let's sit down and talk
And make everything right

By Trancy Custis AKA Tbone Snackz

They Tried To Keep Me Down

I was down, but I'm up again
They tried to stop me but I was born to win
They even tried to take my pride
I hold all the good stuff on the inside
Never let them see the real me
I'm stronger than they will ever be
They talked about me, even put me down
You ain't going to be nothing
Don't come around they said
Yeah, I would get offended by the things people would say
I'm not a follower, I go my own way
I looked into my future and saw some bright things
It's full of surprises and no more pain
I'm a blessed child let y'all should know everything would be alright
I was down but I'm up 'cos God turned all my bad into good
I told God my pain was over, I've been through enough

By Trancy Custis AKA Tbone Snackz

Trying to Overcome All the Pain I Felt

Just sitting here thinking how I used to get in my ways
I want things to be different
Don't want to go through that phase like I was blind
Or couldn't see the things that were getting in my way
Used to go through a lot of problems and some things even hurt
I say no matter what you going through always put God first
I was tired of life, seemed my situation got worst
I never had any luck, felt I like I was under a curse
Even told God about my pains
He said: don't worry about it, everything's going to change

I asked God why things don't feel the same
I felt like giving up
Why is my head down? I can't even hold it up
A lot of stuff on my mind
God, take your hands and wipe away my tears
Protect my body and take away my fears
You made me so You know who I am
Thank you for still keeping me here
You taught me how to forgive and forget
I'm a keep pushing, I can't give up just yet
Having talks with You made me proud
Been doing this ever since I was a small child
Don't have to worry about looking over for that black cloud Ever since I found You, God, I can smile

By Trancy Custis AKA Tbone Snackz

Trying To Overcome the Pain

My heart's pumping; I still don't show no fear
Family that I was close to me don't want me here
It's a proven fact I was down and out
Didn't get any love, what's up with that?
I had to learn the hard way
Had to watch my own back
Still go by Tbone Snackz
They told me if I ever needed something just holler
Why even bother? I made it this far
I had my own dollars
They told lies, even stretched the truth
I've been telling them for years I don't need none of you
I'm being me, what y'all gonna do?
You can talk about me all you want until your face turn blue
What I do with my life is on me, not on you
I'm a one man team don't need a crew

Y'all call yourself my family but you've been putting me down for years
You told me I couldn't make it on my own
Been proving y'all wrong for years
The time I was looking for help I didn't find anyone
I only had myself
But I don't care
All the pain I was holding in
You can see from the tears my decision making wasn't all that right
I'm the only one that controls my life
I got mistreated as a kid but thanks to God
I'm still living life just the way it is
I'm better than that so I'm put out my fingers to the sky and giving my thanks to God

By Trancy Custis AKA Tbone Snackz

Waiting On The LORD To Save Me

Every day of my life I ask God for help on my situation
He knows what kind of dude I am
He knows I ain't got the patience
He can see the pain I'm going through
I had a tough life growing up
If people only knew my childhood wasn't all that great
Brought tears to my eyes when my grandparents left this state
Hard to trust anybody anymore
Gotta watch my back and lean on the Lord t
Thought I already know which one to choose
I can't even think straight, mind getting all confused
Can't even concentrate, the ones that know me can relate
Just got a lot of stuff on my chest
Can't shake everything on my mind
Going to sleep at night without my prayer
I want to go out of this world simply the best

My life has already been put to the test
Hold a lot of stuff on the inside of me, can't let it rest
Why am I going through these pains, beating me up?
I don't know what to do
Just gotta get my head together and my thoughts right
Every situation I faced seem like it done got tight
I'm losing focus, can't even sleep at night
Sitting there waiting on my Lord and Savior Jesus Christ

By Trancy Custis AKA Tbone Snackz

Went Through So Much Pain, Can't Take It No More

Born into this world momma had three mouths to feed
The family had love for my sisters, why not me?
Always feeling left out 'cos I was the black sheep
My two sisters always got love
You've gotta love us all, push comes to shove
I was nothing at all
It built alloy of stress and pain on me
This is some real stuff it ain't a game
Homie, everybody don't know what I'm feeling on the inside
Forget a smile, the only thing I got left is my pride
I'm a take what's left on the inside and forget
Going through this twenty eight years of my life I didn't think I belonged here so tried to end my life
When I got to a certain point in my life I knew I was stronger than that
I got mistreated as a kid, what's up with that y'all?
Tried to keep me down but I always the bounced back
All I'm trying to do is me and get my life back on track
My sisters are going around having fun
My parents did me so wrong
As a kid, how was I their son?

The pain I'm going through nobody else can feel
My life's been messed up and I'm being real
I got treated wrong so what's the deal?
Got cut so deep from the pain
My wounds gotta heal so I keep my faith
As long as I'm here I'll enjoy life the way it is

By Trancy Custis AKA Tbone Snackz

God; I Know U Heard Everything I've been Through

This life I'm living don't even seem fair
With everything I've been through, seemed like nobody cared
Just feels like I wasn't even loved
Family treated me wrong
Nobody to talk too when I was going through my pain
Didn't know what to do anymore, didn't feel the same
Having conversations with God just to ease my pain
Trying to figure out why my life was rough
Every situation I faced seem like it got tough
Don't know what to do anymore, thought I done enough
Life all messed up going through all this stuff
A lot of things done happened to me
I'm standing here now; who knew where I would be
God is who I thank; He carried me
Several times I was left for dead
God didn't want me to leave: that's what His voice said
Just trying to live life day to day; all that negative vibe don't bring my way
The things I've been through didn't think I would be here
God had my back to the whole time; that's why I stayed in gear

By: Trancy Custis AKA Tbone Snackz

Without GOD I Never Would...

Just standing here looking up at the sky
Giving thanks to God for blessing me
I'm still standing here but I don't know why
All emotional with tears in my eyes
I've been through a lot
When I was a youngin' I lost my grand ma and grandpa
Still going through a lot of pain
Like I was lost and everything was about to change
Haters out there still waiting on me getting slain
I'm a believer, that's one thing you can't change
God wanted me so
I'm getting a new life like it just begun
Light so bright like I'm standing under the sun
Still enjoying life 'cos I'm still having fun
I keep praying 'cos still waiting on my son
I'm married now enjoying my life
Twenty years back never thought I would have a wife
Everything was going wrong like I didn't have no life
Had nobody to turn to along the way
People still putting us down
If it wasn't for God a blessing wouldn't be found
Me and my wife are going to do what we gotta do to hold our family down
Haters are going to be haters; we're looking at them now
We can smile now 'cos we're blessed

By Trancy Custis AKA Tbone Snackz

I was Down but God Picked me up

All I'm trying to be is the best
it ain't no competition
I'm not worrying about the rest
Yea, life is hard; ran into a couple of tests
No, I'm not perfect; I go through a lot of stress
Standing there with my cap on
With God written on my chest
Giving all my thanks to Him
For allowing me to still have breath
He's looking at me
Seeing all the things I'm going through
I'm sitting here waiting patiently on my break through
Got my thoughts in my head
'Cos I know what I gotta do
Told the devil: step back 'cos I'm through dealing with you
in my car whispering bad things
God's my healer, He's gonna cure my pains
He heard my call; even heard my name
Stay encouraged is what God told me
You won't feel the same
That's a true saying; now I'm feeling a change
From when I was out there in the world doing evil things
Whole situation is different now; whole life done change
Its feels like I'm different person
I'm still the same dude who needed Christ in my life
If you knew all the things I was going though
Had to give up a lot of my old ways
Starred death in the face twice; I was headed for the grave
I was ready to make something happen
That's why I got saved
Thank the Lord for allowing me to see His Way
And so I thank him each and everyday

By Trancy Custis AKA Tbone Snackz

Why Am I Going Through This

I won't cry now, can't break now
Even if my pain is still around
Can't let my tears hit the ground
Love is all I got, it can be found in Your heaven
Look down on earth, God
I'm doing everything right, how could it not work?
Came into this world straight from birth
Why is all this pain around me?
I'm asking You first
I feel empty like I'm broke
Things are different; I don't understand
I need to come up with something or change my plan
I lay here at night, God, whispering Your Name
Wishing You would come down and fix my pain
Some things are hard; gotta get it go
It's going to hurt, I already know
Thinking about what I did wrong
I can't do this, just gotta stay strong
Can't even smile, just want my life to be complete
Tired of stressing and my heart pacing fast
I'm just hurt from all the pain
Don't want my life to be the same

By Trancy Custis AKA Tbone Snackz

God: Come change Me

God; it feels like I don't belong in this life
It ain't a lot of good things; nothing but bad
How do you sit here and wait on patiently
When everyday of your life you got a different situation?
Tired of going through all the pain
Got a great future ahead of me, so I got everything to gain

Tired of my feelings getting hurt
I'm doing what I can when nothing else works
My hearts torn apart, even brought me to my knees
Prayed to God: Why's everybody hurting me?
All I'm asking for is a change
Things don't feel right anymore, it's not the same
Please come and heal my pain
Just asked myself: Am I liked?
Don't know anymore; tried to take my own life
Hung around nothing but old heads 'cos they give you the best advice
They tell you what's wrong and what's right
Tired of bad luck; God, please fix my life
They always talk about who fears who
I ain't got no one; just shed a lot of tears
The pain I held on the inside been messing me up for years
Ask myself: How long will it last?
I'm hurting too much so it's hard for me to laugh
Three years was stuck in foster care
No family to visit me 'cos they didn't even care
Can't feel my pain if you never been there
I act like I'm alright, who am I kidding?
Just an emotional guy who seems to be holding feelings
I'm on both of my knees praying for a change
Asking God to come and heal my pain

By Trancy Custis AKA Tbone Snackz

You've Gotta Look Out For Yourself

You gotta look out for yourself, nobody else will
A lot of fake people around you so who is real?
I feel so lost right now, like it ain't nothing to do
You keep telling me my attitude stinks
Can you imagine all the pain I went through?
Had nobody to turn to, stood on my own feet

Worried about my own problems, heart never skipped a beat
I done went through the struggle
Keep hearing all this stuff talking about we love you
Hearing nothing but lies
Going back to my old ways
Can't be known as that guy, I done been through the walls
Trying to make something happen when nothing else works
Going in and out of a maze
My life's gonna get better
See myself saying: everything will be okay
There were times in my life had my back against the wall
Choices in both of my hands
Had to make the right call
You're looking at this kid with a lot of ambition
Follow me, listen up and pay attention
I'm in a league of my own where there is no competition
A poem, a writer; so I'm gifted
I'm living life, ain't got to worry about stress
Walking with God now so you know I'm blessed

By Trancy Custis AKA Tbone Snackz

Trying To Enjoy Myself

I'm Trancy Custis, what to do?
Trying to figure out my every move; you don't have a clue
Still wondering? All confused? You should know me; I'm the same dude
Head was all messed up like I'm missing a few screws
People pushing me now, wanting me to flip
Can't let them get to me, got to get a grip
I remember when I used to sit and chill
Listening to people on how they kept it real
No fake people around, that's how I feel
It ain't no competing

Body and life all messed up, I took a beating
I'm a winner so things gotta change
Friends you knew for years turned their backs on you
Spit and said my situation wouldn't change
God, help me go through this stress, I got no strength left
Something good is going to come out of this
And that's a bet!

By Trancy Custis AKA Tbone Snackz

You Were Always There

I need you when I'm going through my pain
Just want you to be there when things ain't the same
Just need someone there when I'm going through
Don't need nobody else, I just need you
I just want to be loved, hold me tight
Give me hugs
You were always there, I can count on you
'Cos you always care
I love you with all my heart
Me and you; nobody can tear us apart
You've been there from the start
Some things don't go my way but you told me:
Everything is going to be okay
When I was asking myself: how long will it last?
Having talks with you made me proud
You brighten my day up
Made me smile, you even wiped away my tears
Told me you weren't going nowhere, you're staying right here
I love you baby cause you still care

By: Trancy Custis AKA Tbone Snackz

I just wanna say "Thank You"

Lord, I just wanna thank you for giving me life
Even though my situations weren't right
I never gave up, every day I had to put up a fight
The devil had me under his wings
Whispering in my ear all the bad things
I thought my world was coming to an end
From all the pain I dropped to my knees
I called out one name –"God"
I know You heard my cries
I want to change, don't want to be known as "that" guy
Couldn't talk to nobody
No one understood my life
Just talking to You, God, made everything alright
You even told me You would forgive me of my sins
I used to smile but they took away my grin
I felt lost; but with God I know I will win
Seemed like no one cared
I was all lonely, that's what I used to feel
But since I found God, I know everything in God is real

By Trancy Custis AKA Tbone Snackz

I'm just trying to find myself

I'm lost right now, trying to find myself
All confused, still lying to myself
Still putting myself in certain situations
A lot of things done happened to me
Thinking about all the stuff I done wrong
I pretty much hate myself
Got a lot of stuff, I just can't shake myself
Always kept my head up, I'm swallowing my pride
I'm still a cool guy, always stood my own ground
You've got to believe me; don't care what you think about me

Take it or leave it
I know when I was young I was mistreated
My attitude gets the best of me
Smoking and drinking put a lot of stress on me
I couldn't understand why I couldn't get love at home
The way I was treated growing up was just so wrong
I didn't talk about it
Just express it in my poems
I smile a lot, who am I kidding?
Just an emotional guy who seems to hide feelings
I'm a grown man now, still feels like I get no love
I'm in the struggle by myself
So I'm continuing to fight the good fight
Trying to fix my situation so I can experience the good life
It feels like I am getting back my senses
Like I've been trapped for years hiding behind fences
I still got a lot of stuff to improve
I'm starting to feel good about myself
I'm going to go out of this world as that cool dude
That's why I'm happy about my life now
Ain't worrying or stressing
'Cos as long as the Lord's in my heart
I'm just waiting on my blessing

By Trancy Custis AKA Tbone Snackz

I'm Looking for Answers

Just walking through the storm and the rain
I'm to forget about my pain
Tears still roll from my eyes
I'm a strong man I can't even cry
Trying to hide all my fears
Wondering why my pain is still following me here
I just want to go to a different place

Why am I going through this?
Trying to hide my face going through life
Like something was still keeping me here
I'm tired of crying, thought I cried my last tear
All I got is me
Don't know where I want to be
My future is right in front of me
My eyes can't see
Looking up in the sky for some help
I need somebody by my side; I can't do it myself
Trying to figure out which way to go
I'm all out of answers, I just don't know
I'm on both of my knees
Begging You to send me a sign
I just need to stop worrying about all the bad times

By Trancy Custis AKA Tbone Snackz

Lord; You Saved Me

I used to live with a lot of sins
Gave up a lot of my old ways to get saved
I thank the Lord for clearing me of my sins
Been through a lot of pain, now I feel blessed again
You carried me through all my rough times
Wiped my tears when I was crying
I remember when I used to get high
Been doing it ever since my grandma died
I thank you from saving me from that life 'cos where I was heading things weren't right
Just sitting alone in the dark with no lights, I'm tired of the devil, I need God in heaven
A lot of things were getting in my way
I want to thank the Lord for every day

By Trancy Custis AKA Tbone Snackz

A Changed Person

Already laid out my plans leaning on the Lord's side
'Cos I'm a blessed young man
Just looking for some different things
Life was all messed up going through the pain
Had a lot of bad luck in my life, faced death at least twice
Just trying to get my life right, feels like I done paid the price
Just looking for some new things
Take away my stress and pains
Don't want my life to be the same
I know You had your angels riding
Tired of having bad dreams about me dying
I got goals I'm trying to reach
Kids in this world that I gotta teach
Mouths to feed they gotta eat
Let me keep my breath 'cos I got to breathe
Just a loving father trying to survive
I get emotional from time to time
Tears rolling down my eyes
Even when I felt weak inside I never gave up
'Cos as long as I have God
I'm going to continue to try

By Trancy Custis AKA Tbone Snackz

Epilogue: Can God Work with U?

The guy was sitting at the bus stop early one morning. He wore a bright orange Tee shirt with matching orange sneakers and his hair was in an afro. A cigarette butt protruded out of the corner of his mouth while he talked on his mobile phone. To some on their way to work he looked like a "loser". As I passed by I heard him telling the person on the other line of his phone how thankful he was that God had caused his creditor to cut his four thousand dollar debt to two thousand dollars. He was grateful they had put him on a payment plan so he could pay his bill in installments. He went on to recount how one of his bills had gotten paid for without his knowledge and he was just oozing praises and gratitude to God. I thought: God can work with that attitude! And then there are some in nice clothes and nice cars, and yet so full of pride in their accomplishments that they have no time for God.

The Lord Jesus said in The Gospel of Matthew, Chapter 9, verses 12 and 13: "But when Jesus heard that, He said unto them, They that be whole* need not a physician, but they that are sick…..for I am not come to call the righteous, but sinners to repentance."** And so the question for each of us is this: <u>Can God work with you?</u>

By Sheila Hayford, Publisher

*In this context the word "whole" refers to those who are well
**This Scripture reference is from the King James Version of the Holy Bible

Thank you for supporting Trancy and Arnita in their writing. God loves you and gifted you like no other. Make time to perfect and share your God given talents. The world needs your gift, use it wisely for the glory of God.

Published by What A Word Publishing and Media Group
www.whatawordpublishing.com

www.ingramcontent.com/pod-product-compliance
Lightning Source LLC
Chambersburg PA
CBHW071725040426
42446CB00011B/2230